The Unseen MBA

Business Fundamentals Learned in the Household

Christopher Michael

BookLeaf Publishing

Presentation by *BookLeaf Publishing*

Web: www.bookleafpub.com

E-mail: info@bookleafpub.com

ISBN: 9789363302723

First edition 2024

Contents

Abstract

Salutation

Preface

Unlock Your Potential: A Guide to Using "The Unseen MBA" Chapters for Growth................................... 1

Identifying Transferable Skills:..................................... 4

How Household Chores Become Your MBA............. 7

Unleash the Hidden Business Leader Within: How Household Chores Become Your MBA................... 7

Surprising parallels between your home and a company... 8

Common Terms or Abbreviations Between a Company and a Household... 10

Household Inventory Types: More Than Just Groceries... 13

A Place for Everything: The Power of Organization in Home and Factory.. 17

The Household Haven..................................... 17

The Factory Flow... 18

Beyond Convenience....................................... 19

Conclusion... 20

Household Inventory Management: A Familiar Parallel to Business Practices................................... 21

Beyond Chores: Household Expenses as a Business Model.. 24

Before We Dive Deeper...................................... 27

Parallels Between a Household and a Company......... 29

Ready to unlock a hidden MBA?............................... 29

From Toddlers to CEOs: The Family Boardroom and Your Future Career.. 36

From Messy Drawers to Millionaires: Why Home Finances Matter More Than You Think............................ 39

From Grocery Lists to Profit Margins: A Household Budget Decoder... 42

The Power of Partnership: Dad (CFO) & Mom (COO) - A Household Leadership Team............................... 45

Leadership.. 48

Servant Leadership: Leading by Serving............... 48

Alignment between Servant Leadership and 10 faces of innovation.. 53

From Factory Floor to Family: Applying Efficiency Concepts at Home.. 57

Unexpected Efficiency Hacks: How Factory Concepts Can Organize Your Home........................... 57

Unconscious Competence........................... 59

Bio-data, Resume, and a CV................................ 61

The Breakdown... 61

Mind Mapping: Unleash Your Creativity and Organize Your Thoughts.. 65

Why is mind mapping important?........................ 65

How can mind mapping help bring ideas to life?.. 66

The Three-Generation Curse of Wealth: Why Riches Don't Last.. 69

About the author.. 81

Abstract

The Unseen MBA unlocks the surprising truth: your household is a powerful training ground for essential business skills. This book reveals the hidden connections between everyday chores and the core principles that drive successful companies.

From budgeting and strategic planning (grocery lists and meal prepping!) to project management (acing that family vacation?) and human resource development (remember those sibling negotiations?), your household experiences are packed with valuable business lessons.

The Unseen MBA equips you to:

- **Identify the hidden MBA skills** embedded in your daily household routines.
- **Translate your household experience** into a competitive advantage in the job market.
- **Master key business terms** using relatable household examples (say goodbye to jargon!).
- **Develop a powerful skillset** that transcends chores and translates to career success.

Whether you're a seasoned professional or just starting out, this book will transform your perspective on household tasks. You'll learn to see them not as burdens, but as opportunities to hone valuable business competencies.

The Unseen MBA: Unveiling the business leader within you, one household task at a time.

Salutation

To life for having taught me that change is permanent. To destiny that taught me to read signs and follow the path to my objectives by setting new goals and targets to cross. To silence for teaching me to collect my thoughts. To the many failures that help me get a little wiser by the day. To be thankful to all who walk with me, pass by me or pass me by on this journey called life. And most of all to the unseen source called God, A Big Thank You!

Christopher Michael ©

Preface

A Lifelong Dream Realized

The seeds of this book were sown in my mind in the mid-80s, fueled by my degree in English Literature and Journalism. I yearned to be a writer, to share my knowledge and empower others. Life, however, had other plans. The daily grind pushed my dream to the back burner, though it never truly died.

Then came the 90s, and an unexpected turn – a career in programming. Driven by a desire to see progress and make things better, I embraced this new path. My programming experience, however, turned out to be a valuable stepping stone. It instilled in me a deep appreciation for the human spirit, our resilience, and our ability to adapt and thrive in the face of adversity. It also gave me a unique perspective on how to interact with technology, a skill that would come in handy much later.

Over time, my notebooks piled up. Walls became a canvas of ideas, plastered with notes and scraps from countless books. I yearned to bring these thoughts to life, to share the wisdom gleaned from experience and experimentation. It was a treasure trove of untrodden paths and unconventional solutions, waiting to be unearthed.

Fast forward to the age of artificial intelligence. As I witnessed the power of Large Language Models (LLMs) like ChatGPT, Copilot, and Gemini, a spark ignited. I saw in them the key to unlocking my treasure trove of notes and ideas.

At age 60, a childlike excitement surged through me. This wasn't just any tool; it was the missing piece I needed to finally write the books that had been simmering within me for decades. Those notes, those papers – they were no longer just scraps, but a goldmine waiting to be unearthed.

With the zeal of a child with a new toy, I delved into the world of AI, learning how to collaborate with Gemini and turn my ideas into a tangible form. Two book ideas emerged, but the first resonated as the most pressing. It wasn't just important to me; it felt like a necessity for the times. So, I took a step back from the second book, a treatise on *Risk and Sustainability for Small Businesses,* and used its insights to shape the first. This first book, *The Unseen MBA,* is a culmination of everything I've learned and experienced.

I'm incredibly excited to share it with you. *The Unseen MBA* isn't just a book; it's the realization of a lifelong dream, a testament to the power of perseverance and the magic of Human-AI collaboration. Thank you for joining me on this journey.

Unlock Your Potential:
A Guide to Using "The Unseen MBA" Chapters for Growth

Here's how a reader can make optimal use of the chapters in "**The Unseen MBA**" for their own growth:

Actively Engage with the Material:

- **Don't just skim:** Read thoughtfully, taking notes on key points and surprising parallels between household tasks and business practices.

- **Think critically:** As you read about "household inventory," "household expenses," or "chores as a business model," reflect on how these concepts apply to your own household.

- **Visualize:** Imagine yourself applying business principles to your daily tasks. How could you be more strategic with grocery shopping or manage your "household budget" more effectively?

Apply the Knowledge:

- **Resume & Interview Prep:** Use the "Common Terms" chapter to translate your household skills into business language for your resume or job interviews. Highlight skills like budgeting, project management (vacation planning!), or team leadership (negotiating chores with siblings).

- **Household Management Transformation:** Utilize the chapters "Inventory Management" and "Expenses as a Business Model" to streamline your household operations. Create a system for tracking household items, reduce unnecessary spending, and make informed decisions about resource allocation (like budgeting for holidays).

- **Career Trajectory Planning:** The chapter "From Toddlers to CEOs" can help you map your career path. Identify skill gaps based on your "family boardroom" experiences and take steps to address them.

Deepen Your Understanding:

- **Discussions & Activities:** Discuss the book's concepts with your family or partner. Have them share their "household CEO" experiences and how they manage tasks. This can spark new insights and shared learning.

- **Real-Life Examples:** As you read about "Dad as CFO" and "Mom as COO," think about the leadership styles at work. Do any similarities exist? Are there leadership lessons you can glean from your family dynamic?

- **Challenge Yourself:** Go beyond the book's examples. Explore other household tasks and see if you can identify additional business parallels. This active engagement will solidify your learning.

By actively engaging, applying the knowledge, and seeking deeper understanding, readers can leverage the chapters in "The Unseen MBA" to unlock their hidden business skills, improve their household management, and ultimately, enhance their career growth.

By Christopher Michael

Identifying Transferable Skills:

Here are some key things you, the reader, should try to assess after reading "The Unseen MBA" to apply the concepts in your daily lives and careers:

What to Assess after reading "The Unseen MBA"

- **Self-awareness:** Reflect on the household tasks and responsibilities you manage regularly. What specific skills do you use to accomplish them (e.g., budgeting, planning, project management, communication, conflict resolution)?

- **Skill translation:** Analyze how these household skills translate to relevant business skills (e.g., budgeting translates to financial management, scheduling a family vacation becomes project management).

- **Building a skills inventory:** Create a list of your transferable skills, highlighting specific examples from your household experiences. This can be used for resumes, cover letters, or professional development conversations.

Actionable Strategies:

- **Highlighting skills in applications:** When applying for jobs, identify opportunities to showcase your transferable skills in your resume and cover letter. Use household examples to demonstrate your abilities (e.g., "Managed a household budget of ₹X, resulting in Y% savings").

- **Preparing for interviews:** Anticipate common interview questions related to relevant skills and prepare answers that showcase your household experiences. Practice weaving in specific examples to illustrate your points.

- **Everyday skill development:** Look for opportunities to further develop your transferable skills through your household tasks. Can you delegate more tasks to leverage leadership skills? Can you implement new planning methods for grocery shopping or family outings to hone your project management abilities?

Mindset Shift:

- **Valuing household work:** Recognize the inherent value of the skills you develop through household tasks. It's not just "chores" – it's practical experience in essential business competencies.

- **Confidence boost:** Understanding your transferable skills empowers you to approach job applications and career advancement discussions with greater confidence.

- **Continuous learning:** View household activities not just as tasks, but as opportunities to learn and grow in areas relevant to your career goals.

By actively assessing your skills, developing strategies to leverage them, and adopting a more positive mindset towards household work, readers can transform "The Unseen MBA" into a powerful tool for career success.

How Household Chores Become Your MBA

Unleash the Hidden Business Leader Within:

How Household Chores Become Your MBA

Ever suspect your parents were secretly molding you for the business world? They were! "The Unseen MBA" unveils the surprisingly powerful connection between everyday household tasks and the fundamental skills coveted in today's business landscape.

This book goes beyond the resume-building experiences of traditional internships. It delves into the hidden curriculum of your home life, revealing how conquering chores and managing a household equips you with the leadership, problem-solving, and strategic thinking valued by top companies.

Surprising parallels between your home and a company

Let's dive right in and map the surprising parallels between your home and a company:

Household Department	Manufacturing Department	Similarities
Finance	Accounting & Finance	Both manage the budget, track expenses (bills vs. raw materials), and ensure financial solvency.
Human Resources (HR)	Human Resources (HR)	Both handle personnel matters, including scheduling (chores vs. shifts), conflict resolution (between siblings vs. employees), and ensuring everyone has what they need (toys vs. equipment).
Marketing & Sales	Marketing & Sales (indirectly)	Both influence buying decisions (grocery list vs. product promotion). Parents influence brands chosen for the household, similar to how marketing influences consumer

By Christopher Michael

		choices.
Operations	Production & Operations	Both manage day-to-day tasks to ensure smooth functioning (cleaning, cooking vs. assembling products, maintaining machinery).
Logistics	Logistics & Supply Chain	Both handle inventory management (pantry vs. warehouse), ensuring the right items are available when needed (snacks for kids vs. parts for production).
Quality Control	Quality Control (indirectly)	Both strive for quality output (clean dishes vs. defect-free products). Parents ensure chores are done properly, similar to quality control checks in manufacturing.

Table: 1.0

Common Terms or Abbreviations Between a Company and a Household

Forget flowery prose - let's get down to business! This section dives straight into the practical connections between common business terms and their surprising applicability to household management. Here are some common terms or abbreviations that can be connected between a company and a household.

Finance & Accounting:

- **Budget:** Both companies and households create budgets to allocate resources and track expenses.

- **ROI (Return on Investment):** Companies measure the return on investments, while households can consider the "return" on investments in things like energy-efficient appliances (saving money on electricity bills).

- **P&L (Profit & Loss):** While companies aim for profit, households can track their "profit" as the amount left over after all expenses are paid.

Operations & Logistics:

- **Inventory Management:** Both companies and households need to manage inventory (stock in a warehouse vs. food in a pantry). Techniques like FIFO (First In, First Out) can be used in both settings.

- **Logistics & Supply Chain:** Companies manage complex supply chains, while households manage a simpler version – ensuring they have the necessary supplies on hand (cleaning products, toiletries).

- **Project Management:** Both companies and households can use project management skills to tackle tasks (renovation project vs. planning a family vacation). This involves setting goals, timelines, and delegating tasks.

Human Resources (HR):

- **HR:** Both companies and households can be seen as having "HR" functions. This includes managing schedules (chores vs. work shifts), delegating tasks, and resolving conflicts (between siblings vs. employees).

- **Teamwork:** Both companies and households rely on teamwork to function smoothly. Parents work together, and siblings share responsibilities, similar to how teams collaborate in a company.

Marketing & Sales (indirectly):

- **Marketing:** Companies use marketing to influence buying decisions. In a household, parents influence the brands chosen for groceries and household items, similar to how marketing influences consumer choices.

- **Sales:** While not directly selling products, households make purchasing decisions, considering factors like price, quality, and brand (similar to a company's sales considerations).

Other Common Terms:

- **CEO (Chief Executive Officer):** In a household, parents can be seen as the CEOs, making overall decisions and managing the household.

- **CFO (Chief Financial Officer):** The person managing the household budget can be seen as the CFO.

By Christopher Michael

- **KPI (Key Performance Indicator):** Companies use KPIs to track progress. In a household, KPIs could be things like good grades (for children) or staying within budget.

By understanding these common terms and how they apply to both companies and households, you can see how many skills learned at home are directly transferable to the professional world.

Household Inventory Types: More Than Just Groceries

While managing a household might not seem like running a business, there are surprising parallels between the two. One key area of similarity lies in inventory management. Let's delve into the commonalities between household and company inventory types.

The Unseen MBA: Business Fundamentals Learned in the Household

By Christopher Michael

Inventory Type	Household Example	Company Example	Similarities
Raw Materials	Flour, sugar, vegetables (for cooking)	Chemicals, Lumber, steel, fabric (for manufacturing)	Both are base components used to create finished products (meals vs. manufactured goods).
Work in Progress (WIP)	Half-prepared meals, ingredients measured out for a recipe	Partially assembled products, unfinished components	Both represent items in various stages of completion before becoming a final product.
Finished Goods	Ready-to-eat meals, packaged snacks	Completed products ready for sale or use	Both are final products ready for consumption or use (meals for family vs. products for customers).
MRO (Maintenance, Repair, & Operating Supplies)	Cleaning supplies, light bulbs, batteries	Tools, office supplies, safety equipment	Both are items used to maintain the overall functioning of the household/company (cleaning supplies vs. tools) and ensure smooth operations.

Table: 1.1

Email: realtime.ventures@gmail.com / chris@albizin.com -
"Triggering Thought" Books

- **Lead Time:** Both households and companies need to consider lead time when managing inventory. This refers to the time it takes to receive an item after placing the order (e.g., waiting for groceries to be delivered vs. waiting for raw materials to arrive from a supplier).

- **Inventory Management Techniques:** FIFO (First In, First Out) can be used in both settings to ensure older items are used before they expire (food in a pantry vs. raw materials in a warehouse).

- **Inventory Control:** Both households and companies need to track inventory levels to avoid stockouts (running out of essential items) or overstocking (wasting money on unnecessary items).

Key Differences:

- **Scale:** Company inventories are typically much larger and more complex than household inventories.

- **Inventory Turnover:** Companies often aim for a higher inventory turnover rate (selling inventory quickly) compared to households.

- **Cost Management:** Companies have a greater focus on cost management when it comes to inventory, considering factors like bulk discounts and supplier negotiations.

In conclusion, while the scale and complexity may differ, both households and companies deal with similar inventory management principles to ensure they have the right items available at the right time

A Place for Everything: The Power of Organization in Home and Factory

The adage "**a place for everything, and everything in its place**" isn't just a neat saying; it's a cornerstone of efficient living and successful operations. From the organized kitchen pantry to the well-stocked factory floor, order creates a ripple effect of benefits.

The Household Haven:

Imagine a kitchen where spices reside in a jumbled mess, pots and pans clatter in overflowing drawers, and forgotten ingredients lurk in the back of cabinets. This disarray not only wastes time searching but can also lead to food spoilage and wasted money. Here's where the power of designated spaces and clear labelling comes in:

- **Organized drawers and cabinets:** Divide drawers with organizers for utensils, separate spices in labelled containers, and employ stackable shelves to maximize vertical space.

Email: realtime.ventures@gmail.com / chris@albizin.com -
"**Triggering Thought**" Books

- **Labeling is key:** Clear labels on containers and shelves instantly communicate what's where, saving time and frustration.

- **Declutter regularly:** Parting with expired items and unused gadgets creates a more manageable space.

The Factory Flow:

The same principles that streamline your kitchen extend to large-scale operations like factories. Inventory management becomes crucial to ensure smooth production and avoid costly delays. Here's how organization translates to the factory floor:

- **Designated bins and shelves:** Specific bins and clearly marked shelves ensure parts and materials are readily accessible to production lines.

- **Inventory control systems:** Just like labeling your pantry, barcodes and digital tracking systems provide instant information on stock levels and locations.

- **Minimizing hazards:** Disorganized storage can create safety hazards by blocking walkways and obscuring potential dangers. A well-organized factory floor promotes safety and efficiency.

Beyond Convenience:

The benefits of organization go beyond just saving time and frustration. They have a significant impact on:

- **Safety:** A cluttered environment is a recipe for accidents. Clear storage practices minimize tripping hazards and ensure easy access to safety equipment.

- **Efficiency:** Knowing exactly where items are located allows for faster retrieval, leading to increased productivity in both home and factory settings.

- **Reduced waste:** Proper organization helps identify and eliminate expired or unused items, saving money on both groceries and factory supplies.

Conclusion:

Taking the time to create a designated space for everything, and ensuring everything is in its place, yields a multitude of benefits. From the tranquility of a well-organized kitchen to the smooth operation of a factory floor, order promotes efficiency, safety, and a sense of calm control over our environments. So, embrace the power of organization – it's a philosophy that applies to all aspects of our lives.

Household Inventory Management: A Familiar Parallel to Business Practices

Ever rummage through your pantry, only to realize you're fresh out of milk or detergent? It happens to the best of us! But this everyday experience highlights a hidden skill you might not even realize you have **inventory management.**

Think about it – your home is a **mini-warehouse** filled with its own unique inventory. Just like **businesses**, households need to keep track of what they have, plan for future needs, and store things efficiently. Here's a table that compares household and workplace inventory, with a bonus cost column to see if you can estimate your own household's "**operating budget**":

The Household Inventory Table:

Category	Types of Inventory	Estimated Cost
Cleaning Supplies	Laundry detergent, fabric softener, dish soap, dishwasher detergent, all-purpose cleaner, disinfectant wipes, toilet cleaner, bathroom cleaner, glass cleaner, floor cleaner, sponges, rags, trash bags	
Clothing & Footwear	Clothes for different seasons and occasions, shoes, boots, sandals, undergarments, sleepwear, activewear (for some households)	
Decorations	Artwork, pictures, plants, throws, pillows, candles	
Electronics	TVs, computers, laptops, tablets, smartphones, gaming consoles, speakers, headphones, chargers	
Food & Beverages	Canned goods, dry goods (pasta, rice, flour), spices, condiments, baking supplies, fresh produce, dairy products, frozen food, beverages (coffee, tea, juice, etc.)	
Furniture	Beds, couches, chairs, tables, dressers, bookshelves, lamps	

The Unseen MBA: Business Fundamentals Learned in the Household

By Christopher Michael

Kitchenware & Cookware	Pots and pans, baking sheets, casserole dishes, mixing bowls, spatulas, whisks, knives, cutting boards, utensils, can openers, measuring cups and spoons	
Lightbulbs & Batteries	Different types of lightbulbs for various fixtures, batteries of various sizes	
Linens & Bedding	Sheets, pillowcases, blankets, duvets, towels, washcloths, bath mats	
Medicine & First Aid	Pain relievers, allergy medication, cold & flu medication, digestive aids, bandages, antiseptic wipes, thermometer	
Paper Products	Toilet paper, paper towels, napkins, facial tissues, printer paper, paper plates, plastic wrap, aluminum foil	
Personal Care	Shampoo, conditioner, soap, body wash, toothpaste, deodorant, shaving cream, razors, makeup, skincare products, feminine hygiene products	
Pet Supplies	Food, treats, toys, bedding, leash, collar, poop bags, litter (for cat owners)	
Stationery & Office	Pens, pencils, markers, notebooks, paper clips, stapler, tape dispenser,	

Email: realtime.ventures@gmail.com / chris@albizin.com -
"Triggering Thought" Books

Supplies	Printer cartridges	
Tools & Hardware	Hammer, screwdrivers, wrench set, tape measure, level, pliers, toolbox, nails, screws	
Vehicle	Cleaning agents and tools for maintenance	

Table: 1.2

Beyond Chores: Household Expenses as a Business Model

Running a household requires many skills, and financial management is a crucial one. Interestingly, the expense categories you juggle at home may have surprising parallels to how companies manage their finances.

The Household Expenses Table:

Category	Description	Estimated Cost
Children's Expenses	Childcare (if applicable), diapers/wipes (if applicable), school supplies, extracurricular activities (sports, music lessons, etc.)	
Clothing & Footwear	Clothes, shoes, accessories for all family members	
Debt Payments	Student loans, car loans, credit card debt (minimum payments), personal loans	
Entertainment	Streaming services, movies, hobbies, vacations (occasional)	
Food	Groceries, dining out (occasional)	
Healthcare	Doctor visits, Health insurance premiums, co-pays, prescriptions	
Housing	Rent or mortgage payment, property taxes, homeowners insurance (if applicable), utilities (electricity, water, gas, trash)	
Insurance	Health insurance, life insurance (optional)	

Linens & Bedding	Sheets, pillowcases, blankets, duvets, towels, washcloths, bath mats	
Miscellaneous	Phone bill, internet service provider, haircuts (adults), laundry detergent, household cleaning supplies, gifts, personal subscriptions	
Personal Care	Clothes, toiletries, cosmetics, haircuts	
Pet Expenses	Food, vet care, grooming (optional)	
Savings & Retirement	Contributions to savings accounts, retirement plans	
Transportation	Car payment (if applicable), car insurance, gas, public transportation (if applicable)	
Utilities	Electricity, water, gas, trash removal, internet	

Table: 1.3

Before We Dive Deeper

Before We Dive Deeper: Take a moment to pause and reflect. Have you ever considered the hidden connections between your home life and the world of business? Perhaps while tackling a mountain of laundry, you don't realize you're honing project management skills. Or maybe that grocery list you meticulously craft is a testament to your budgeting prowess.

This section of "The Unseen MBA: Business Fundamentals Learned in the Household" delves into these surprising parallels. We've explored:

- **Surprising parallels between your home and a company**: Unveiling the hidden similarities between household tasks and the fundamental skills valued in business.
- **Common terms or abbreviations:** Connecting the dots between familiar terms used in both households and companies.
- **Household inventory types:** Going beyond groceries to reveal how managing your pantry mirrors inventory control practices.
- **Household inventory management:** Highlighting the connection between keeping your home

stocked and the principles of business inventory management.

- **Beyond chores: household expenses as a business model:** Demonstrating the way you manage your household finances is akin to a company's financial planning.

Get ready to expand your mind! Prepare to see your everyday household tasks in a whole new light – as powerful training grounds for essential business skills.

Parallels Between a Household and a Company

Ready to unlock a hidden MBA?

Ready to unlock a hidden MBA? Look no further than your own home! Those everyday tasks you juggle might surprise you – they are powerful training grounds for essential business skills. Let's delve deeper into these surprising parallels between a household and a company:

Strategic Planning:

- **Household:** Long-term goals involve things like saving for a house, children's education, or retirement. Planning involves considering future needs and allocating resources accordingly.
- **Company:** Setting long-term goals for market share, profitability, or product development. Strategies involve analyzing the market, competition, and internal resources.

Strategy:

- **Household:** Deciding between buying a house or renting, choosing between public or private

school for children. These choices impact long-term financial goals.
- **Company:** Deciding between entering a new market, developing a new product line, or acquiring another company. These strategies define the company's direction.

Planning:

- **Household:** Creating a budget to allocate income towards expenses, groceries, and savings goals.
- **Company:** Developing financial forecasts, production schedules, and marketing plans to achieve strategic objectives.

Finance & Accounts:

- **Household:** Tracking income (salaries) and expenses (bills, groceries), managing savings and debt.
- **Company:** Recording financial transactions, managing cash flow, preparing financial statements like income statements and balance sheets.

Human Resources Management (HRM):

- **Household:** Dividing chores and responsibilities among family members, managing conflicts, and setting expectations.
- **Company:** Recruiting, hiring, training, and motivating employees, fostering a positive work environment.

QA & QC (Quality Assurance & Quality Control):

- **Household:** Ensuring chores are done properly (clean dishes, folded laundry), redoing tasks that don't meet expectations.
- **Company:** Setting quality standards for products or services, inspecting products to ensure they meet those standards.

Sales & Marketing:

- **Household:** Negotiating allowance with parents, convincing siblings to share toys, advocating for desired purchases.
- **Company:** Promoting products or services to potential customers, and creating marketing campaigns to increase sales.

Supply Chain Management:

- **Household:** Maintaining a well-stocked pantry with groceries, ensuring enough supplies (toiletries, cleaning products) are available.
- **Company:** Managing the flow of materials from suppliers to production facilities, and ensuring timely delivery of finished goods to customers.

Procurement:

- **Household:** Making informed buying decisions (comparing grocery prices, searching for deals), purchasing necessary items.
- **Company:** Sourcing raw materials and supplies at the best possible cost and quality, establishing purchasing procedures.

Product Development:

- **Household:** Creating new recipes, experimenting with different cleaning methods, finding creative ways to entertain children.
- **Company:** Developing new products or services, innovating existing products, researching and testing new technologies.

Maintenance:

- **Household:** Performing regular maintenance on appliances and vehicles, fixing leaky faucets, mowing lawns.
- **Company:** Maintaining equipment and machinery to prevent breakdowns, ensuring smooth production operations.

Operations:

- **Household:** Managing the daily tasks of running a home, ensuring meals are prepared, laundry is done, and the house is clean.
- **Company:** Transforming inputs (raw materials, labor) into outputs (finished goods or services), ensuring efficient production processes.

Production:

- **Household:** Preparing meals (cooking), cleaning the house, completing chores – these are all forms of "production" within the household.
- **Company:** The core function of a company is production – manufacturing goods or providing services.

Human Resources Development (HRD):

- **Household:** Encouraging children to learn new skills, providing opportunities for them to develop their talents and interests.
- **Company:** Investing in employee training and development programs to enhance their skills and knowledge.

Total Productive Maintenance (TPM):

- **Household:** Preventive maintenance like cleaning appliances, organizing closets, and decluttering regularly to maintain order and efficiency.
- **Company:** A proactive approach to maintenance that focuses on preventing equipment failures and maximizing production uptime.

SWOT Analysis:

- **Household:** Strengths (reliable income, organized family), Weaknesses (disagreements, time constraints), Opportunities (learning new skills), Threats (unexpected expenses, job loss). Understanding these factors helps make informed decisions.

- **Company:** Analyzing internal Strengths and Weaknesses, along with external Opportunities and Threats, are crucial for strategic planning.

External Environment:

- **Household:** Factors like rising food costs, changes in work schedules, or a neighbor's renovation project can all impact a household.
- **Company:** Economic conditions, political developments, technological advancements, and competitor actions are all external factors that affect a company.

From Toddlers to CEOs: The Family Boardroom and Your Future Career

Here's how a household can be seen as a parallel to company growth and how roles evolve:

Early Stages: The Startup Family

- **Board of Directors (BoD):** Mom and Dad are the ultimate decision-makers, setting the overall direction (budget, discipline) and allocating resources (chores, allowances).
- **Management:** Young children may have minimal responsibilities but begin to learn basic tasks and contribute in small ways.

Growth Phase: Expanding Responsibilities

- **Board of Directors:** Parents delegate more authority as children mature. Shared decision-making is introduced (meal planning, household projects).
- **Management:** Children take on more complex tasks (cooking simple meals and managing their rooms). They may even develop supervisory roles over younger siblings, assigning chores and ensuring completion.

Expansion Phase: The Evolving Family "Company"

- **Board of Directors:** As children become young adults, parents transition to an advisory role. Collaborative decision-making becomes the norm (financial planning for college, household budgeting after children leave home).
- **Management:** Young adults manage their own schedules, contribute financially, and may even take on leadership roles within the household (planning family vacations or coordinating schedules).

IPO (Initial Public Offering) or Leaving the Nest

- Children eventually leave home, establishing their independence. The "family company" may restructure, with parents focusing on their own retirement goals

Conclusion:

The family dynamic mirrors a company's growth stages remarkably well. It highlights how early experiences with responsibility, teamwork, and leadership translate into valuable skills for navigating the professional world.

From Messy Drawers to Millionaires: Why Home Finances Matter More Than You Think

The Household CFO: Why Numbers Matter at Home

Just like companies rely on sound financial management to thrive, households need a grasp of bookkeeping, accounts, and financial planning. Here's why:

- **Planning for the Future:** Financial goals like saving for a dream vacation, a child's education, or retirement all require budgeting and tracking expenses. Without a plan, unexpected expenses can derail your dreams.
- **Avoiding Debt Distress:** Impulse purchases and uncontrolled credit card use can quickly spiral into financial stress. Proper budgeting and tracking expenses can help you avoid debt traps.
- **Informed Decision Making:** Understanding your income and spending habits empowers you to make informed financial choices. Should you buy a new car or invest in your future? Financial awareness helps you prioritize.

The Thin Line: Success vs. Breaking the Bank (For Companies and Households)

Both companies and households face similar risks when it comes to financial management:

- **Living Beyond Your Means:** Companies overspend on projects or have poor sales, leading to bankruptcy. Similarly, households exceeding their income through excessive spending can face financial ruin.
- **Lack of Financial Planning:** Companies without a financial roadmap struggle to adapt to changing markets. Households without a budget and savings plan are vulnerable to unexpected financial blows.
- **Poor Cash Flow Management:** Companies with poor cash flow management can't pay their bills. Households facing the same issue struggle to meet their basic needs.

Conclusion:

Effective financial management is the cornerstone of success for both companies and households. By taking control of your finances, setting goals, and making informed decisions, you can navigate the path towards financial security. It all starts with good bookkeeping, clear accounts, and a well-defined financial plan – your "homegrown MBA" for a prosperous future.

From Grocery Lists to Profit Margins: A Household Budget Decoder

Ever feel like your grocery list prep is a mini-MBA lesson in disguise? You're not wrong! This exploration delves into the surprising world of household budgeting, revealing how the skills you use to manage your family's finances translate directly to the world of business.

From strategically allocating resources (meal planning!) to tracking expenses (those pesky receipts!), your everyday budgeting battles are equipping you with powerful financial management skills. This chapter acts as your decoder ring, deciphering the common budget-related terminology used in both households and companies.

Get ready to unlock the hidden meaning behind terms like "fixed costs" and "return on investment," all through the familiar lens of your household budget. Prepare to see your grocery list in a whole new light – as a powerful training ground for essential business skills!

The Budgeting Table

Household Term	Company Term	Definition
Income	Revenue	The total amount of money received from salaries, allowances, or other sources (household) or from sales of goods or services (company).
Expenses	Costs	The total amount of money spent on various items like groceries, utilities, and entertainment (household) or on raw materials, salaries, and rent (company).
Budget	Financial Plan	A roadmap outlining expected income and expenses over a specific period (month, year) for both households and companies.
Fixed Expenses	Fixed Costs	Expenses that remain constant each period, like rent, mortgage payments, utilities (household) or rent, salaries, loan payments (company).
Variable Expenses	Variable Costs	Expenses that fluctuate depending on usage, like groceries, entertainment (household) or raw materials, travel expenses (company).
Savings	Retained	Money set aside for future goals,

	Earnings	emergencies, or investments (household) or profits not distributed to shareholders and reinvested back into the business (company).
Debt	Liabilities	Money owed to creditors, like credit cards or loans (household) or money owed to suppliers or banks (company).
Budget Deficit	Net Loss	When expenses exceed income in a given period (household) or when a company experiences a loss (negative profit).
Budget Surplus	Net Income	When income exceeds expenses in a given period (household) or when a company experiences a profit (positive income).

Table: 1.4

The Power of Partnership: Dad (CFO) & Mom (COO) - A Household Leadership Team

Similarities to a Company:

In a well-run company, the Chief Financial Officer (CFO) and Chief Operating Officer (COO) work in close collaboration, not competition. This is also true for a household managed by a "**Dad-as-CFO**" and "**Mom-as-COO**" model. Here's why:

- **Shared Goals:** Both the CFO and COO—Dad and Mom in this case—share the ultimate goal of a successful and thriving household.
- **Complementary Skills:** The CFO focuses on financial strategy and resource allocation, while the COO oversees daily operations and ensures smooth execution. Similarly, Dad might manage the budget and investments, while Mom takes charge of day-to-day tasks like scheduling, logistics, and ensuring everyone's needs are met.
- **Communication & Collaboration:** Regular communication and clear division of responsibilities are key to success. Dad and Mom need to discuss financial plans, adjust budgets

based on operational needs, and make joint decisions for the household's well-being.

Why Clashing Roles are Detrimental:

- **Confusion & Inefficiency:** Conflicting priorities or unclear roles can lead to confusion and inefficiency. For example, Dad might prioritize long-term savings over immediate needs, causing friction with Mom who manages day-to-day expenses.
- **Reduced Morale:** When parents constantly disagree on financial decisions or operational approaches, it can create tension and negatively impact the overall family dynamic.
- **Missed Opportunities:** Without a collaborative approach, the household might miss opportunities to optimize finances or streamline operations.

Effective Partnership:

- **Defined Roles & Responsibilities:** Clearly defining financial and operational responsibilities helps avoid overlap and promotes clarity.
- **Open Communication:** Regular discussions about finances, plans, and challenges are crucial

for making informed decisions and aligning
goals.
- **Mutual Respect**: Respecting each other's skills
and contributions fosters a positive partnership.
- **Flexibility & Compromise:** Being flexible and
willing to compromise on certain aspects allows
for a more balanced approach.

Conclusion:

The Dad-as-CFO & Mom-as-COO model can be
highly effective as long as both parties work
collaboratively. By leveraging complementary
skills, open communication, and respect, they
can create a thriving household that functions
much like a well-oiled company.

Leadership

Servant Leadership: Leading by Serving

Servant leadership is a leadership philosophy that prioritizes the well-being and growth of those being led. It flips the traditional leadership model on its head, where the leader is seen as the one in charge of giving orders.

Note: *The word "servant" in "servant leadership" can sometimes be misinterpreted as having a derogatory connotation. This is because the traditional meaning of "servant" implies a subordinate role. However, in servant leadership, the term "servant" is used differently. It refers to a leader who prioritizes the needs of their followers and empowers them to achieve their full potential.*

Here are the core principles of servant leadership:

- **Focus on Others:** Servant leaders prioritize the needs and aspirations of their followers over their own.
- **Empowerment:** They create an environment where followers feel empowered to take

ownership, make decisions, and reach their full potential.

- **Growth & Development:** Servant leaders invest in their followers' growth by providing opportunities for learning and development.
- **Empathy & Listening:** They exhibit empathy and actively listen to understand their followers' needs and concerns.
- **Building Community:** Servant leaders foster a sense of community and collaboration within the team.

Benefits of Servant Leadership:

- **Increased Engagement:** Employees feel valued and invested in the success of the organization.
- **Improved Decision-Making:** Diverse perspectives and empowered employees lead to better decision-making.
- **Enhanced Innovation:** A culture of growth fosters creativity and innovation.
- **Stronger Retention:** Employees feel supported and are more likely to stay with the organization.

Examples of Servant Leaders:

- **Nelson Mandela:** Empowered his followers to fight for equality in South Africa.
- **Martin Luther King Jr.:** Inspired millions through his commitment to social justice.
- **Indra Nooyi (Former CEO of PepsiCo):** Known for her focus on employee development and sustainability.

Becoming a Servant Leader:

Servant leadership is not a title, but a way of being. Anyone can develop these qualities by practicing empathy, listening actively, empowering others, and fostering growth within their teams.

Servant Leadership Beyond the Workplace: Examples in Homes and Communities Servant leadership isn't confined to office spaces. Its core principles can be practiced anywhere, including within families, friendships, and even broader communities. Here's how:

Among Siblings:

- **The Older Mentor:** An older sibling patiently teaches a younger one how to ride a bike, prioritizing their learning and enjoyment over personal time. (**Focus on others, development**)
- **The Conflict Mediator:** When siblings argue, one sibling steps in, listens to both sides without judgment, and helps them find a solution collaboratively. (**Empathy, listening, building community**)
- **The Supportive Friend:** One sibling encourages and celebrates the other's accomplishments, genuinely happy for their success. (**Empowerment**)

Among Friends:

- **The Organizer:** A friend takes the initiative to plan a group outing, considering everyone's preferences and ensuring everyone feels included. (**Focus on others, building community**)
- **The Emotional Support:** A friend listens attentively to a friend going through a tough time, offering a shoulder to cry on and emotional support. (**Empathy, listening**)

- **The Skill Sharer:** A friend who excels at a particular skill (coding, playing music) offers to teach their friend, investing in their growth and development. (**Empowerment, development**)

In Society:

- **The Community Volunteer:** Someone volunteers their time and skills to help those in need, putting the community's well-being above personal gain. (**Focus on others**)
- **The Environmental Advocate:** An individual organizes clean-up drives and educates others about environmental issues, prioritizing the well-being of the environment and future generations. (**Focus on others, development**)
- **The Uplifting Mentor:** A mentor provides guidance and support to a younger person, helping them navigate challenges and reach their full potential. (**Empowerment, development**)

These are just a few examples. Servant leadership can show up in countless ways, as long as the core principles of prioritizing others' growth, empowerment, and well-being are present.

Alignment between Servant Leadership and the 10 Faces of Innovation:

The 10 Faces of Innovation, a concept developed by innovation expert Tom Kelly, outlines ten different personality types that contribute to the innovation process. Here's how these faces can blend with servant leadership to create a powerful force for positive change:

The 10 Faces of Innovation

The Learning Personas

1. **The Anthropologist:** Servant leaders actively listen and understand the needs of their teams. This aligns with the Anthropologist who observes and gathers insights to inform innovation.
2. **The Experimenter:** Servant leaders encourage calculated risk-taking. This supports the Experimenter who tests and iterates on ideas.
3. **The Cross-Pollinator:** Servant leaders value diversity and inclusion. This fosters an environment where the Cross-Pollinator can bring together different perspectives for innovation.

The Organizing Personas

4. **The Hurdler:** Servant leadership focuses on overcoming challenges collaboratively. The Hurdler role is about individual resilience in the face of obstacles.
5. **The Collaborator:** Servant leaders prioritize teamwork and shared decision-making. They foster a collaborative spirit, which is essential for the Collaborator role.
6. **The Director:** Servant leaders provide guidance and do not simply delegate tasks. This can be helpful for the Director who sets the overall direction while empowering the team. However, a strong servant leader might avoid being too directive and focus more on guiding or pointing.

The Building Personas

7. **The Experience Architect:** Servant leaders prioritize creating a positive work environment. This can indirectly support the Experience Architect who designs a positive innovation journey for the team.
8. **The Set Designer:** Servant leadership teaches one to appreciate one's physical environment

and look at opportunities or possibilities within the now.

9. **The Storyteller:** Servant leaders use compelling narratives to inspire and motivate their teams. Storytelling is a powerful tool for the Storyteller to communicate the vision and purpose behind the innovation.

10. **The Caregiver:** A core tenet of servant leadership is putting the needs of others first. This aligns perfectly with the Caregiver who ensures the well-being and psychological safety of the team during the innovation process.

Benefits of Blending the Two:

- **Enhanced Innovation:** By incorporating the diverse strengths of all ten innovation faces, servant leadership fosters a more creative and innovative environment.
- **Sustainable Change:** Servant leaders, with their focus on people and empowerment, can ensure that innovative solutions are implemented effectively and have a positive impact on those involved.
- **Broader Appeal:** By incorporating different perspectives and approaches, servant leadership-driven innovation can be more

inclusive and appealing to a wider range of stakeholders.

Conclusion:

Servant leadership creates a fertile ground for innovation to blossom. By embracing all ten innovation faces and fostering a collaborative environment, leaders can drive positive change and achieve remarkable results.

From Factory Floor to Family: Applying Efficiency Concepts at Home

Unexpected Efficiency Hacks: How Factory Concepts Can Organize Your Home

The concepts of Just-in-Time (JIT), Overall Equipment Effectiveness (OEE), and Kanban can be applied to homes to a certain extent, but they wouldn't be used in the same way as factory settings. Here's a breakdown:

JIT at Home: How to Minimize Waste and Save Money

Just-in-Time (JIT): This is about minimizing storage space by only buying what you need, when you need it. In your home, this could translate to things like:

- Making a grocery list and sticking to it to avoid impulse purchases.
- Planning meals to avoid food waste.
- Only buying clothes or furniture for a specific purpose.

However, unlike factories that rely on precise deliveries, homes often face unexpected needs. So, a fully JIT approach might not be realistic.

Kanban for Chaos: Streamlining Your Home Life with Visual Tools

Kanban: This is a visual method for managing work in progress. In your home, a Kanban board could be used for:

- Keeping track of chores or to-do lists.
- Organizing tasks for a project (e.g., home improvement).

Kanban boards help visualize workflow and identify bottlenecks, but they wouldn't be as critical in a home environment as they are in production lines. Overall, these concepts can inspire you to be more organized and efficient in your home, but they'll likely need to be adapted to fit your specific needs and lifestyle.

Overall Equipment Effectiveness (OEE)

This measures how efficiently equipment is used in manufacturing. In your home, this could be applied loosely to appliances. For instance:

- Regularly maintaining appliances to prevent breakdowns and extend their lifespan.
- Using appliances only when needed (e.g., not running the dishwasher half-empty).

However, OEE is a more complex metric used in industrial settings and wouldn't be directly applicable to everyday home appliance use.

Unconscious Competence

People often develop these skills intuitively in their daily lives without realizing they're using formal methods like JIT, OEE, or Kanban.

- We avoid overstocking groceries to prevent waste (JIT).
- We take care of our cars to avoid breakdowns (OEE).
- We use mental to-do lists to prioritize tasks (Kanban).

Transferable Skills: Highlighting these "unconscious" skills on a resume demonstrates transferable abilities valuable in the workplace.

- Planning and prioritizing (Kanban)
- Resourcefulness and cost-consciousness (JIT)
- Preventative maintenance (OEE)

By making this connection, you can showcase your ability to apply these concepts effectively, even outside a formal work environment. This demonstrates a well-rounded skill set that can be adapted to professional situations.

Here's an example:

"While managing my household, I've unconsciously applied **Just-in-Time** principles by minimizing impulse purchases and planning meals to reduce food waste. This translates to strong budgeting and resource management skills that I can bring to your team." So, framing these everyday practices as transferable skills can absolutely strengthen your resume and showcase your adaptability.

Bio-data, Resume, and a CV

The Breakdown

Here's a breakdown of the differences between bio-data, resume, and CV, along with their etymology and usage:

Bio-data (short for biographical data):

- **Etymology:** "Bio" from Greek "bios" (life) and "data" from Latin "datum" (something given).
- **Usage:**
    - → Primarily used in South Asian countries for job applications, government positions, or research grants.
    - → May also be used for marriage proposals in some cultures (including personal details).
    - → Can be similar to a resume or CV, but often includes more personal information like date of birth, religion, marital status, and other information generally omitted from resumes/CVs.

Resume (French word meaning "summary"):

- **Focus:** Concise document summarizing your work experience, skills, and education relevant to a specific job application.
- **Length:** Ideally one page, sometimes two, depending on experience level.
- **Content:** Highlights achievements, quantifiable results, and skills tailored to the job description.
- **Usage:** Most common document used for job applications in North America and many other countries.

Curriculum Vitae (CV) (Latin meaning "course of life"):

- **Focus:** Comprehensive document detailing your entire academic and professional history.
- **Length:** It can be multiple pages, depending on your experience and accomplishments.
- **Content:** Includes education, research experience, publications, awards, and detailed work experience (including all positions held).
- **Usage:** Typically used for **academic positions, research grants, or highly specialized fields.**

Why it's important to understand the difference:

- Using the wrong document can create a negative impression on potential employers or grant reviewers.
- A resume should be targeted and relevant, while a CV can be more comprehensive.
- Understanding the regional variations in terminology (bio-data) can ensure you're using the appropriate documents.

The Breakdown Table

Feature	Bio-Data	Resume	Curriculum Vitae - CV
Etymology (Origin)	Bio (Greek) + Data (Latin)	French	Latin
Focus	Personal & Professional Info	Work Experience & Skills	Entire Academic & Professional History
Length	Varies	1-2 pages	Multiple pages
Content	Personal details, Education, Work Experience (sometimes)	Skills, Achievements, Tailored to Job	All Education, Research, Work Experience, Awards
Usage	Job Applications (South Asia), Marriage Proposals	Most Job Applications	Academic Positions, Research Grants, Specialized Fields

Table: 1.5

Mind Mapping: Unleash Your Creativity and Organize Your Thoughts

Mind mapping is a visual brainstorming technique that helps you organize information, generate ideas, and connect concepts in a non-linear way. It's like creating a roadmap for your thoughts, allowing you to see the big picture and the relationships between different details.

Why is mind mapping important?

- **Boosts Creativity:** Mind maps encourage free-flowing thinking, helping you break through mental blocks and generate new ideas.
- **Improves Organization:** By visually laying out information, mind maps help you organize complex concepts and identify the relationships between them.
- **Enhances Memory:** Visual cues like colors, images, and keywords trigger memory recall more effectively than plain text.
- **Increases Focus:** Mind maps help you stay focused on a central topic while allowing you to explore related ideas without getting sidetracked.

- **Promotes Collaboration:** Mind maps are a great tool for brainstorming sessions and group projects, allowing everyone to contribute and see the connections visually.

How can mind mapping help bring ideas to life?

- **Develop a project plan:** Use mind maps to break down a large project into smaller, manageable tasks.
- **Organize research findings:** Visually connect key points and sources from your research.
- **Plan a presentation or speech:** Structure your content and identify key points you want to convey.
- **Write creatively:** Generate ideas for stories, poems, or essays through mind mapping.
- **Solve problems:** Identify root causes and brainstorm potential solutions visually.

Here are some resources to get you started with mind mapping:

- Tutorials:

    - https://www.lucidchart.com/pages/how-to-make-a-mind-map

- **Mind Mapping Software (Free and Paid Options Available):**

    - XMind (https://xmind.app/)
    - Miro (https://miro.com/)
    - Coggle (https://coggle.it/)

By developing your mind mapping skills, you gain a valuable asset for brainstorming, organizing information, and bringing your ideas to life in a creative and impactful way.

Example of the Power of a Mind Map

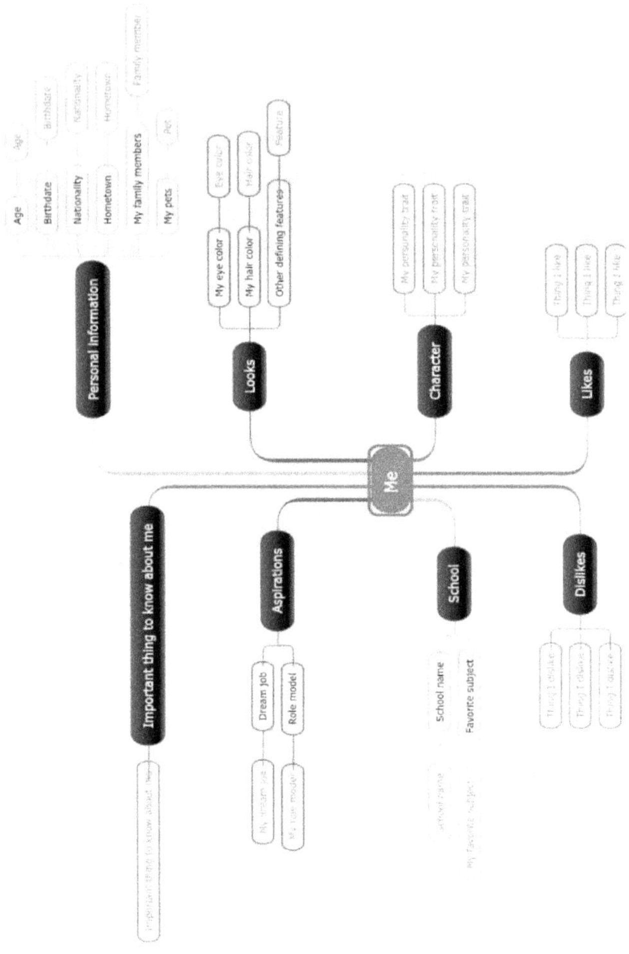

The Three-Generation Curse of Wealth: Why Riches Don't Last

As the saying goes, '**from shirtsleeves to shirtsleeves in three generations.**' This means that wealth accumulated by one generation is often lost by the third generation. Why does this happen and what can be done to prevent it. Understanding the three-generation rule is crucial for anyone who wants to build and preserve wealth for their family. By learning from the mistakes of others, we can ensure that our hard-earned wealth lasts beyond our lifetime and benefits future generations.

First Generation: The Builder

The first generation of wealth, also known as the builder, is typically the hardest working and most determined of the three generations. They often start with very little and through sheer grit and perseverance, they accumulate wealth over their lifetime. Builders are risk-takers and entrepreneurs who are not afraid to put in long hours and make sacrifices to achieve their goals. They have a clear vision of what they want to accomplish and are willing to do whatever it takes to get there. Their success is often a result of their ability to identify opportunities and take advantage of them before anyone else.

Second Generation: The Maintainer

The second generation, also known as the maintainer, plays a crucial role in preserving the wealth created by the builder. While the builder works hard to accumulate wealth, it is up to the maintainer to ensure that this wealth is protected and grows over time. This requires a different set of skills than those possessed by the builder, including financial management, investment strategies, and risk assessment. The maintainer must also be mindful of the potential pitfalls that can threaten the family's wealth, such as overspending, poor investments, and family conflict. They must work diligently to maintain the family's financial stability and ensure that the wealth created by the builder is passed down to future generations. Without the careful stewardship of the maintainer, the family's wealth may not last beyond the third generation.

Third Generation: The Squanderer

The third generation, also known as the squanderer, is often the downfall of wealthy families. They are born into wealth and have never experienced the struggle that their ancestors faced in creating it. As a result, they may lack the work ethic and financial responsibility necessary to preserve the family's wealth. The squanderer may spend extravagantly on frivolous items or engage in risky investments without fully understanding the consequences. They may also fail to plan for the future and neglect to invest in education or philanthropy. Without proper guidance and education, the third generation can quickly deplete the family's wealth and leave nothing for future generations.

The Cycle of Wealth

The cycle of wealth is a phenomenon that has been observed throughout history. It starts with the first generation, who typically accumulates wealth through hard work and determination. The second generation then takes over, tasked with maintaining the wealth created by the first generation. However, the third generation, often referred to as the squanderer, tends to waste the wealth created by their predecessors. This cycle can repeat itself indefinitely, leading to the downfall of wealthy families. One reason why this cycle occurs is due to a lack of financial education. Without proper guidance, subsequent generations may not have the knowledge or skills to manage the family's wealth effectively. Additionally, entitlement and family conflict can also contribute to the downfall of wealthy families. It's important to recognize these factors and take steps to prevent them from causing irreparable damage to your family's wealth.

Lack of Financial Education

One of the biggest contributors to the downfall of wealthy families is a lack of financial education. Without a solid understanding of how money works and how to manage it effectively, even the most successful families can quickly find themselves in financial trouble. This is especially true for those who inherit wealth without having to work for it themselves. A lack of financial education can lead to poor decision-making when it comes to investments, spending, and overall financial planning. It can also lead to a sense of entitlement and a lack of appreciation for the value of hard work and perseverance. Ultimately, this can result in the loss of wealth that was built up over generations.

Entitlement

Entitlement can be a major factor in the downfall of wealthy families. When children grow up with a sense of entitlement, they may not develop the skills and work ethic necessary to maintain their family's wealth. They may also make poor financial decisions, assuming that their family's money will always be there to bail them out. To avoid this, it is important for parents to instill a sense of responsibility and work ethic in their children from a young age. They should encourage their children to pursue education and career goals, rather than relying on family wealth. Additionally, parents should set clear expectations and boundaries around financial support, so that their children understand that they are not entitled to unlimited resources.

Family Conflict

Family conflict is a common issue that can contribute to the downfall of wealthy families. When family members disagree on how to manage their wealth or have different priorities, it can lead to tension and even legal battles. In some cases, family members may even resort to sabotaging each other's efforts to preserve the family's wealth. To prevent family conflict from ruining the family's wealth, it's important for family members to communicate openly and honestly with each other. They should establish clear guidelines for managing their wealth and make sure everyone is on the same page. It's also important to have a neutral third party, such as a financial advisor or mediator, who can help resolve conflicts and ensure that everyone's interests are taken into account.

Estate Planning

Estate planning is a crucial aspect of preserving wealth for future generations. It involves the creation of a comprehensive plan that outlines how assets will be distributed after death, as well as strategies for minimizing taxes and avoiding probate. Without proper estate planning, a family's wealth can quickly dissipate, leaving future generations with little to nothing. One key component of estate planning is the establishment of trusts, which can help protect assets from creditors and ensure that they are distributed according to the wishes of the deceased. Another important consideration is the use of life insurance policies, which can provide a source of income for surviving family members and help cover estate taxes. Overall, estate planning requires careful consideration and expert guidance to ensure that a family's wealth is preserved for generations to come.

Philanthropy

Philanthropy is an important aspect of preserving wealth for future generations. By donating money to charitable causes, wealthy families can not only make a positive impact on society, but also instill important values in their children and grandchildren. Additionally, philanthropy can help mitigate some of the negative effects of extreme wealth concentration, such as social unrest and political instability. By using their resources to address pressing societal issues, wealthy families can help to create a more equitable and just society for all.

Investing in Education

Investing in education is one of the most important ways that wealthy families can ensure their wealth lasts beyond three generations. By providing access to high-quality education, families can equip future generations with the tools they need to succeed in life and avoid the pitfalls that often lead to the squandering of wealth. Education helps to instill a strong work ethic, critical thinking skills, and an appreciation for the value of money. It also provides opportunities for personal growth and development, which can lead to fulfilling careers and a sense of purpose in life. By investing in education, families can help break the cycle of wealth and create a legacy of success that lasts for generations to come.

Family Values

Strong family values and a work ethic are essential for ensuring the success of future generations. When children grow up in an environment where hard work and dedication are valued, they are more likely to adopt these traits themselves. This can lead to a cycle of success that lasts beyond three generations. However, instilling these values is not always easy. It requires parents and grandparents to lead by example and actively teach their children the importance of hard work, responsibility, and respect. This can be challenging in a world where instant gratification is often prioritized over long-term goals.

Breaking the Cycle

Breaking the cycle of wealth is no easy feat, but it can be done. One of the most important steps in breaking the cycle is to instill a sense of financial responsibility and education in future generations. This means teaching children and grandchildren about budgeting, investing, and saving for the future. It also means encouraging entrepreneurship and hard work, rather than relying solely on family wealth. Another key factor in breaking the cycle of wealth is to avoid entitlement and lavish spending. Families should create a culture of humility and gratitude, and focus on using their wealth for a positive impact in their communities and beyond. This can include philanthropy, investing in education, and supporting local businesses and causes.

Case Studies

One example of a wealthy family that successfully broke the cycle of wealth is the Rockefeller family. Despite being one of the wealthiest families in history, they have managed to preserve their wealth for over six generations. One key factor in their success was their strong emphasis on philanthropy and giving back to society. By investing in education, healthcare, and other social causes, they have not only preserved their wealth but also made a positive impact on the world. Another example is the Pritzker family, who founded the Hyatt hotel chain. They have been able to maintain their wealth for over four generations by diversifying their investments and creating a family office to manage their finances. They also place a strong emphasis on family values and education, ensuring that future generations are equipped with the knowledge and skills to manage their wealth responsibly.

Conclusion

In conclusion, the three-generation rule is a concept that explains why wealth tends to dissipate after three generations. The first generation, the builder, accumulates wealth through hard work and determination. The second generation, the maintainer, preserves the wealth created by the builder. However, the third generation, the squanderer, often wastes the wealth created by the previous generations. This cycle of wealth can be broken through financial education, philanthropy, investing in education, instilling strong family values and work ethic, and proper estate planning.

It's important to understand this concept because it can help families avoid the downfall of their wealth and ensure that it lasts beyond three generations. By taking proactive steps to preserve their wealth, families can create a legacy that will benefit future generations and society as a whole.

Resources

For those who are interested in delving deeper into the topic of wealth preservation, there are a number of resources available that can provide valuable insights and strategies. One excellent resource is the book *The Three Generation Rule: Understanding Why Wealth Lasts Only Three Generations* by James E. Hughes Jr., which provides a comprehensive overview of the topic and offers practical advice for preserving wealth over multiple generations. Another useful resource is the website of the Family Firm Institute, which offers a range of educational materials and resources for families seeking to preserve their wealth and legacy. The site includes articles, webinars, and other resources that can help families navigate the complex challenges of intergenerational wealth transfer.

About the Author

Christopher Michael shatters the mold of traditional educators. A champion of the **unyielding human spirit**, he ignites curiosity and empowers individuals through a concept he calls "**Thought Ignition.**" This approach equips people to simplify their lives and ultimately contribute to a better society.

Fueled by a diverse intellectual fire, Christopher's passions span philosophy, technology, economics, and innovation, all fueled by a deep concern for human well-being. He's keenly aware that many people stop actively seeking knowledge after college and entering the workforce. This, coupled with the demands of

Email: realtime.ventures@gmail.com / chris@albizin.com -
"Triggering Thought" Books

parenting, creates a **knowledge gap** in our rapidly evolving world.

Christopher believes this stagnation hinders parents and can lead their children to doubt their capabilities. A lifelong learner himself, he champions the power of continuous learning. His mission is to bridge this **gap and reignite the excitement of learning and innovation** for people of all ages.